My Secret Muse

My Secret Muse

by

Brandon Tezzano

Grey Dawn Publishing

ISBN: 979-8-9870468-0-7

Cover design by Grey Dawn Publishing.
Book design by Grey Dawn Publishing.

Printed by Grey Dawn Publishing, in the United States of America.

First printing edition 2023.

www.greydawnpublishing.com

Dedicated to

My Secret Muse

Table of Contents

My Secret Muse

Spring Equinox

I.

The longer you focus on keeping a secret
the harder it becomes to finally say it out loud.
The secret wants to keep living quietly inside of you,
burrowing into the ventricles of your heart,
scurrying around inside your veins.
It doesn't want to be forced into the dangerous world
outside.
Real life is scary, for a secret – you see,
before a secret is told to anyone, it is very small and
fragile
like a beautiful insect, wings glistening like gossamer
and an easily-crushed body colored like a precious
gem.
My secret has lived safely inside my heart for a very
long time.
Whenever somebody says your name,
whenever I see your face, especially, I feel it
startle, and burrow even deeper into my chest,
out of a fear of being discovered,
of being hurt.

II.

Her roses wail
From their hard, mottled leaves,
Showing that she has borne many blossoms
Through this maw of ash and flesh,
And now, like them,
There is only the tree of wisdom
From which she has finally escaped
The howl of a black storm.

III.

By and by it all stopped again.
I plucked the last rose from its stem,
tore off the silky petals.
They are each a part of me.
The warmth of them is what I carry.

Wildness can't be tamed, it must come free.
As if with the rose petals, I leave my body behind,
relinquishing life and the desire to survive.
My life to live is to dance to the magic of wildness.

The last scents: rose, oil
and spring, bitter almond
and grass, smell of new grass.

To walk, one last time, and now I'm free.
The wind blew, and I was lost.

When I returned
from the rose fields
I was a different body.
The heart was another place.
Now there are flowers, and grass,
and roots in this new body.
The whole earth.

IV.

I hum with the birds in their gardens.
I have written you out of the harvest.
I imagine your tread
The same heave as the oar of my heart.
You are with me no longer.
The sun moves on the wall.
Fatal rays of the graven tongue
That talks amongst the shadows
In their resting places.
It's a watch I keep,
Because your skittish shadow lags.
You stopped your watch some two centuries ago.
I, what is now mine, must keep it.
It is the poison I breathe.

V.

To be beautiful without ever being seen,
To fly in an atom without wings.
A potted orchid sits
On my desk, caught in a gauze of green.
A mirror of loss.

I sit in the limey air
And look at myself, at the door,
I look at my fingers
Smearing mud and blood.
I am
Waiting for a gyre
Of discords
To vanish
Or for a shooting star
To start a blaze in the dark sky.
And then, one after another,
I see them.
I see you.
I hear the sounds
Of our bodies,
The gasping and the giggling,
The shrieking of the showers
Falling over us in a torrent.
The wind picking up in a thunderous roar
And, above all, the heartbeats.

VI.

In the deepest forest
you sing to the trees,
singing down to their dark-tangled roots
and up to their twisted limbs,
fingertips reaching up to scrape the sky.
They wrap around your words,
hold them close,
strangle them until
they don't even come close
to resembling what they used to be,
these twisted remnants buried
deep under the wet earth.
Deep-reaching tendrils into the
compartments of your pounding heart
which is as good as a living
wooden treasure chest that
you keep locked against
anybody who comes knocking.
Something that has a keyhole
but was designed
without a key.
You spend hours alone
running your fingers over
your splintered edges
and then sanding them down,
sanding it down,
sanding it down.

VII.

I crafted the image of myself like a god
making the first man out of clay.
I smoothed myself out, flawless,
no imperfections in my skin.
My clay self was malleable, a quick learner:
Do this. Don't do this. Try that.
          Despite all of this,
my flawless clay man was not perfect enough for you.
You found it too easy to crush him under your heel,
leave him marred,
still striving to put himself back together
in a way that you could love.

VIII.

Between a chandelier of shattered shards
And a cellar door, I lie in a bed of soft dirt.
Far below a wind of rain trills
Like the air blowing over mountains.
I sleep for a day or two
Or try to.
It's less frightening than it's ever been.
I watch myself drifting;
It's what you do when you're dead.
To face each sunrise as the last,
Without ever having seen its source.
The tiles are naked
In every facet
Of an empty, empty universe.

IX.

The first time our bodies touched
(I still remember it. Your chest to my ribcage.
Sudden, electric.)
a reaction took place, an exchange of
electrons. A transfer of energy
that changed my chemical formula
into something science had never seen before.
In awe I imagined seeing sparks fly,
a change in color,
a sparkling precipitate collecting.
My test-tube heart bubbled over.
I became someone new, a person I had never met,
tied to you by the atoms we now shared.
My neurons rewired to yours in a chemical response,
you could read my thoughts
before I even had them.
The flask changes color.
The heart swells.

X.

At the Bacchanalia
we spun and danced
the firelight licked our skin
and turned it golden.
The small hairs on your arms
stood on end, glowing like
cherry-red coals.
I remember it in waves,
in flickers and small fragments.
Someone's teeth glossy and
shining in the half-light,
white incisors and two square
front teeth like seashells.
Rising voices braiding together,
a pack of wolves at the moon;
I can't remember what
we were trying to hunt.
There was red wine in anything
but a wine glass, poured sloppily
into mason jars,
old glass milk bottles,
drunk with a straw. Smeared
blood replaced by wine-red.

I dipped two fingers in the mason
jar and used it to paint my face,
something dark and different
from another time.
I wanted to look crazed, crazy.

We wanted to watch something
catch flame and
then burn up (or burn down).
What did we pick?
        I know the answer, but
I'm not allowed to say.
I won't think about it too much.
Over the smaller flames
we burnt smaller offerings.
A ring of sapphire that filled the
air with pale blue fumes,
a piece of bread with cheese,
a page from a book,
I think it was from the Old Testament.
It wasn't mine.
Things that the gods would
scoff at, if they were
even looking. More likely
they turned a blind eye to us in
our embarrassing emulation of
them in another life.

You spat on one of the
coals just to watch it bubble,
someone touched their finger to
it just to feel it sting.
The problem with doing that
is that it is very intentional,
very human. Acting
godlike was a choice, which is
the least godlike thing of all.

XI.

Metamorphosis;
a new person who climbed
out of the old skin the day you
moved out of home. Left your
childhood house as a dog-eared book
you would open for nostalgia
but never read again.
Your cells all turned themselves
inside out, organs replenished
themselves. Healing is ugly
sometimes, scabs to itch at,
not as beautiful as hurting sometimes
seems. The yellowed soft pages
of memory are left open, words
faded by the cruel light.

XII.

What they don't tell you is
growing hurts;
the push of plants through the soil,
the steady ache of teething,
horns pushing through the tender skin of a
forehead like a perpetual migraine.
Growth is penetrating and sometimes damaging.
It provides a small hurt, or sometimes
even a large one,
only able to be fixed with time.
What they don't tell you is that
growing still hurts
even long after you have lost
your last baby tooth.

XIII.

Sometimes greater than the pain of
an experience is the pain that
you are alone in your experience of that thing,
that horrible, isolating thing.
One of the greatest components of pain is
the loneliness it drags in with it
like a cat providing its owner a misguided gift.
A soul in pain sees itself as alone.
Your soul, seeing the words of a
suffering poet from centuries ago,
breathes a sigh of relief that it is not
the first to suffer this way.
That past poet reaches through time and
space and pages to bandage the wound
that has been left in you.
But why does mine never heal?

XIV.

The foxes run,
through the long damp grass,
over muddy hills
through the shallows,
leaping over
and squirming under.
They are so flame-bright
that they hurt to look at.
I'm sorry that when
you needed me,
you saw me
out there amongst
their amber and rust,
disappearing over the horizon,
impossibly fast.
I am only at home where
nobody can find me,
where nobody can run
fast enough to catch me.
The foxes run
and crows circle
overhead, calling,
questioning.
Nobody answers.

XV.

See all the little ways in which the
world heals itself, even urban and polluted,
even when not what we would call
beautiful.
In the blistered sidewalk cracks there are
weeds growing but they still reach
their faces to the sun and flower.
Lizards lose their tails to the cruel
world's claws and slowly they grow a new one
that has never known pain.
Abandon a house and the world reclaims it
with moss on windows, unconventional carpeting,
vines climbing the walls and cracking them.
The world pushes forward;
the world keeps pushing through.

XVI.

When she fell from heaven
she broke all of her bones,
every last one.
Even the three in the inner
ear, the ossicles,
so tiny that they look
as if they were from a
hummingbird.
She landed in a wet
hollow of mud and grass,
landed like a meteor,
surrounded by a
filthy halo burnt into
the ground.
It rained that night
and under the water
that covered her,
she slept,
breathing the water
as if it were air.
All of her bones healed,
even the ossicles.

XVII.

I spread my guilt out
onto a platter,
luxuriously, carelessly,
and then I picked it up
between my
index finger and thumb
and swallowed it whole.
Guilt should
taste bitter, sour,
leave my lips puckered
and my mouth dry.
I should lie to you
and say that it was,
but alas, my
guilt is gone now.
There is no reason to lie;
it slipped down my
throat sweetly and smoothly.
It tasted like honey.
I barely had to swallow.

XVIII.

Those men change, as often as they want.
Their bodies abide by no calendar.
Like androids. That's their plan,
And I hear it when I stand on the empty hill
And listen to the breeze through a covered mouth.
A bell shakes up my bones.
Finally, I understand your life:
Because it's nothing, it may always be nothing.

Summer Solstice

I.

You froze all winter and then
burned all summer.
I wish you were embarrassed of it;
this glaring sensitivity to
any change in your surroundings.
It shines off you like an aura.
       Like a mirage over
a hot road, tar pooling and
dripping, sticking to shoes.
What I am trying to say is
that everyone who touches
you comes away
       covered in something
they can't quite scrub off.

II.

There may have been other people to love
but why would this matter to me?
The lack of extraordinary would be
a horrible failure.
With you, there is a current
that runs between our bodies,
a string of fairy lights,
bright and hot to the touch;
the tender burn on my fingertips
is still better than
lukewarm love.
As a by-product of this chemical
reaction we may produce poison,
heat, even the burning cold of
ice that makes a lover's fingertips
yellow, but no matter.
We further science;
the test of human endurance.
How far I am willing to go to experience
something outside of mediocre.

III.

I bade farewell to the flutes
Of those whom I have failed.
To understand the sound of words
Of this life, that you thought so merrily out of joint
Like the wind whistling at the empty moat.
I sink the teeth of my own tongue into the sands
Of time without you there to dwell.
O you I conjure to steal the eyes of the
Blue Lady, the banshee of the Hymn to Nike,
Who should violate you with flaccid canals of pink.
But now, nevermore do I want
To whisper in the smooth grave
In a night when you keep
Snakes in an empty cistern.
My guts are drowned in your hours.
My lips pinch in laughter as the midnight clay
Falls from your forehead
Into a pile of gossip.
Strange, but the sentence
I dreamed of you, which was to blow
Out upon the frozen river
Follows me even now, across space and time.
My summers are now spent in your ghosts.
The thing I conjured to me was a kind
Of crystalline fatality, which
Strewed your lies across the horizon.

IV.

As she lay alone, I was already upon her.

You were so lovely then.

In the morning, I heard voices
and the hour when you were to rise, past your call,
I came out from the depths of a vault
into sunlight,
already you loved me
and you followed me
through the stormy streets of the city,
across the frozen shore and up the slope,
up the trees into the hollows of their roots,
into your heart
and I had come,
for your sea had inspired
my sea.
You had come for your sea,
and if you fail me,
then at least
I will not fail you.

V.

The price of love is a type of undressing,
an agony of being exposed,
completely vulnerable.
An isopod's hard shell removed
to expose its tender inside
to sharp beaks and cruel claws.
Love costs removal of layers,
peeling back,
a skinned rabbit,
a raw beating heart.

VI.

My mother stretched her hands out to me,
a rough piece of driftwood, a willow,
swaying in the sea's pull,
gripping me for balance, waiting.
You grabbed my fingers when I crept near,
when you were alone.
A large hand,
then a smaller hand of crag and bone.
You smelled of ocean.

I played inside my mother's rooms,
staring through windows at the empty islands,
a new and fascinating sight,
lost in wonder as she watched over me,
then hurled me into the waves for my own safety.
I have no sisters to play with now.
I have no brothers. I have no brothers.
And no place to run.
Now, not even the blank pages of your book
can hold me.

VII.

Listening for life that always dies, but seldom hears.
Listening for life that never dies.
Learning to live forever in a body that ceases to live.
Learning to die in a heart that becomes dead.
Listening for death that never dies.
Listening to time for a skeleton to come
and move this cold earth into a lapping tide.

Kill the trees that move the skies
and blood is their summer song.
Blood is their blood in time and here,
red and brown and white.

This hearkens down this lonely gravel road,
down these cold lanes,
those darkening desert nights.
The white moon half-filled in the day,
and the desert's heart the same dark stain
in the white moon,
and on either shoulder three scrawny crows,
their bodies drawn up against a sudden aching
of dying trees and rising sky,
their wings stretched against the night
like pale feathers.

VIII.

There is an intense vulnerability in two hands
intertwined, it is always some kind of pleading;
      Stay with me
      Understand me
      Please notice everything that lies within me
and within my human hands, their veins full of color
and flesh full of heat, my palms pressed together like a
kiss or a curse or a promise.
      I will complete a circuit, my own electricity.

IX.

In ancient Greece you fed me grapes by hand,
fed me stories that I ate,
your voice sweet in my mouth.
My heart was wine-stained, wine-drunk.

I was your gladiator, fought lions for you,
always knew where to find your eager face in the stands
so that I could press my bloody fingers to my lips
        and send you a kiss,
there in front of everyone.

In Medieval times we were prosecuted,
I remember that much, the daughter of aristocracy
and a peasant boy.
             "How can you love him?"
they asked of you, and I asked it too.
You just returned that gladiator kiss I sent you
centuries ago, and that was enough of an answer
for me.

We were lovers in Paris, black coffee on
street corners and when you twirled,
the city dust caught in your striped skirt.
        I proposed where the Eiffel Tower would
        one day be.

I have chased you through lifetimes,
and you have chased me;
a give-and-take,
push-and-pull.
I suppose now it is my turn to chase,
now that I have found you again in this one.
Don't you remember me?
Your gladiator, your peasant,
your French paper boy?
If you don't love me back, in this lifetime,
I will see you in the next one.

X.

Slow mornings half-asleep
aching to reach out,
gnawing monkey-brain wanting
to grab at your knee, your shoulder,
the half-hidden crown of your
head to check that
you hadn't dematerialized somehow.
I must have dreamed
that I woke up alone but
it never made itself reality.
This neurotic checking
is the price I pay for not being
able to go to sleep touching
anyone else, for having
to curl up alone in
the coolest part of the bed.

XI.

"I love this song," you told me,
so I listened to it more critically than
usual, taking note of each change
of pitch, collection of notes, each small
melody, wondering:
is this why she likes it?
has she noticed this part, too?
Whenever I hear it now, I imagine
a particularly sultry note tugs at
a string tied somewhere in my chest,
and you feel an echoing tug in yours.
My heartstrings and yours vibrate
to the same frequency now, the
same low C minor.
When, in silence and alone,
I feel the tug, I know
that you have heard that note,
and thought of me.

XII.

Untarnished love morphs as soon as
it is over. The affair,
the confession, the moment when
two amorphous bodies disengage
from each other, amoebae separating
into two wholes.
How good something is
becomes defined
by how they are remembered,
not how they were in the moment.
In your memory, every
word and moment take up
a different shape
like a coat-rack in the shadows.
(Is there a monster in the corner
of my room? Is it watching me?)
Once it was over,
we became something frightening.
Something that has horns
and sharp teeth, and isn't afraid
to use them (or afraid
of anything).
I wish I could scuba-dive
down to those moments
in the sweet void where they existed
unsullied by our future.

That narrow cave, a difficult
passageway to squeeze into.
But whenever I try
to go there, my air supply
runs out and I become dizzy and
sick with carbon dioxide poisoning.
My pupils blow to the size
of small moons, I moan
and twist and spent eight
days in the hospital.
One time I got close enough
to glimpse a flicker of
something; I don't know
what, your dress in
the sun, your hand in mine
with your nails perfect
clean ovals.
I rested my hand on
the wall of the cave and the
rock cut clean through,
red spiraling up.
A call to sharks,
a sign of fresh meat.
I clamped the wound shut,
ascended to the surface.

XIII.

On your skin, constellations
I mapped out once with a pen.
Gave them names, tried
to be fancy and do some in
Latin; gave up and did them in
English instead.
Inside of wrist, the Dolphin.
Clear as day, the two points of its
tail, the laughing mouth
tasting your skin, tasting my
fingertip when I touched so gently.
On your left shoulder,
the Gemstone. Thought of a joke
about putting it on your left finger
instead, then thought
better of it
         for now.

XIV.

We had neon lights printed on the
walls, nothing quite like a girl
laughing, head thrown back
to damp stains on the ceiling.
Brutal ponytail, brutal neckline.
People who can't feel their own
heartbeat like a bassline that beats
as if it has its own pulse. That is
one thing that she knows for sure.

XV.

I didn't want to hurt you,
just wanted to see if
you'd bleed when cut.
I know it sounds stupid,
but I didn't think you would.
Your skin was so tanned
that I couldn't see the
veins underneath, roped
with defined muscles.
The tiny hairs on your
forearms were bleached
golden by the sun. They
barely cast a shadow.
Looking at the firm outer
barrier between your insides
and the rest of the world,
I managed to convince
myself that you were the
least fragile person I had
ever met. That you would
not shatter when dropped
or feel pain when broken.
I didn't even think I could
break the skin; I thought the
knife would break instead.

Have you ever seen
something so beautiful that
your response is to try and
figure out how to destroy
it? The diligent scientist
slicing open peacocks,
luminescent butterflies,
slick koi fish. Blue blood
in veins, brain coiled up
like some sleeping creature.
Beauty cannot withstand
this kind of onslaught, this
kind of terror. The thing
about dissections for the
sake of discovering beauty
to take for yourself, is that
the result is so much uglier
than how you were before
you started to slice, what
little knowledge you had
of beauty dissolves inside
of your body, and worst of
all, the creature pinned to
the table in front of you has
never been less beautiful
or less alive.

XVI.

What you are in love with is
not love itself, or the act of loving,
or even the concept of romance.
You have always wanted to exist
entirely in the moments before love begins,
in the doubt of returned feelings.
You think that you long for others,
but this moment you want to live in
shows that what you long for
is the act of longing for them, the act
of pining and hoping and wondering.
Even in love, you yearn for longing.
That is your own love affair.

XVII.

When the eye of the world cracks open,
I will watch as it severs the flesh of your body,
the color draining from your lips
like clouds in the face of a summer storm.

I am in my power now.
I will be in my power with every word I say.

With every word I speak, I am taking you.

This world is a monster's nightmare;
I see it in bright and violent colors.

Her eyes rolled to the back of her head;
she knew that this would be her death.

Autumn Equinox

I.

On the day the moon blocked out the sun,
the world shriveled underneath
the halo it left behind.
For a moment, the sun,
having spent so many years carefully
tending to the plants and animals,
forsook its duties.

On the day the moon blocked out the sun,
onlookers gathered to point and marvel.
How amazing it was that something
so constant could disappear from view
if only for a lingering moment
of abandonment.

On the day the moon blocked out the sun,
across countries and districts,
every creature touched by this strange
shadow shivered at once.

A cold feeling across the spine.
A reminder of how perilous it is
to rely entirely
on something other than yourself.

II.

In the pure hollows of the pine
and the rich song of the night,
Time will call up the living dead,
and there is no safety for them.
All our great deeds in the heavens
will have made us outcasts.
For we are haunted
by the voices of our shadows
and the ghosts of our sacrifices.
The sight of the Earth
is a curse upon us.
I forget to bow my head
when I pick out a star in the clear sky.
Time dissolves the feather in my hand.

III.

The witches add
rosemary for love,
longevity, milkweed
for doubt, for longing
that poisons.
The pot bubbles, brims,
turns incandescent
violet, gold, rose-water
pale pink, deep magenta.
They sprinkle sage for
cleansing and spiritual
energy, dogwood for
death and life and
rebirth which is at its
essence the perfect
marriage of the two.
It sticks tar-black
to the bottom of
the cauldron, scraped
free with a stake that
once split a child
clean in two.
Next comes a whole
heart, still desperately
beating, although nobody
says to whom it belongs.

It dissolves in seconds,
something completely
insubstantial, sea foam
and dandelion fluff.
Lavender, for blue
and green, serenity
stillness and calm.
The boiling stops,
the bubbles cease,
the potion clears.
They ladle it into pots
and pans and mugs and
bottles and jars and
ornate china teacups.
The witches drink
their love, their doubt,
their death and life.

IV.

There was a point where I was
lost in the doors and hallways
of the haunted house, where I
began to forget what the streets
outside looked like. What my
own familiar home looked like.
All I could remember suddenly
were shadows, corners, dark
spaces and light stained dirty
orange. Nooks that nightmares
could burst out of, skeletons
crumbling out of closets, a new
and inventive horror behind
every closed door. Under my
nervous feet, patches of floor
boards would collapse into dust
and I would be left with my
leg hanging through the floor,
feeling like bait being dangled
into the deepest part of the sea.
Rats scuttled. I would turn
a corner and be plunged into
total darkness. I couldn't even
remember what light looked like
without being married to the fear
of the absence of it. I mean that

I couldn't allow myself to enjoy
anything, because it made it so
much worse when it was gone.
And it was always gone again.
What did it feel like to be warm
without being entirely too hot,
without feeling like my skin was
full of a thousand burning ants?
I stumbled on, mirrors and trap-doors,
bathroom taps that turned
on all by themselves. Bats in the
attic, spiders in the bedsheets. In
the haunted house, I asked the
thick grey walls if I had ever
known happiness before or
if I had just always imagined it
for myself. I asked if I had ever
lived somewhere else, in the warm
home I so distantly remembered,
but never waited for an answer
because the alternatives were so
frightening. That I had always
lived here. Always lived here
alone. That I was born inside the
haunted house. That all I was
was this haunted house.

V.

In the center of a love song I will lay my body down, my tired bones and the ache in my feet from trying to wear shoes that were the wrong size and always have been. I will collapse in on myself more with every note, every word that reminds me how it feels to feel, and I will keep collapsing until I am small enough to slide under a door like a love letter, small enough to get lost under the refrigerator for 2 years until you move and I am discovered. I want to package myself away safely into a reality that I have composed on my own, so that I will never have to know what it feels like to miss you. Slot into your pocket like some spare change, unobtrusive and useful.

VI.

I sit and watch you.
My limbs enraptured by my vision,
And I feel a red wind pass along my gut,
As you run your fingers along yours.
I feel a lightness inside that is desperate,
And out of your flesh I grab a molder of thought.
How do you keep the human in the animal
From the animal in the human?

VII.

The cup of coffee went
cold, lost all its heat
to the empty room around it.
Thermodynamics is
cruel in this way,
sucking energy ruthlessly
in shameless pursuit of
an equilibrium
that will never be met.

VIII.

She undressed herself in the
corner of my room,
the one furthest away
from the harsh glow of
the street lamp that
flowed through
the open curtains.
It illuminated her anyway,
caught bright on her
edges, like a flame
licking at a piece
of parchment.
She took her halo off
first, picked pieces
of baby-hair free
from it, slid
it softly off the curved
crown of her head.
She laid it on my
bedside table, smoothly,
softly, ready to be
put back on as
soon as possible.
It gave off its
own unsettling glow

when removed from
her; a cold glow,
like an empty airport
or train station at
5 in the morning,
populated only by those
with absolutely
nowhere else to go.
Watching that
divine light spilling
helplessly into my bedroom,
I ached with want and
fear, undiluted.
Next she reached
behind her back,
behind her delicate shoulder-blades.
I remembered, when I was
young, my mother referring
to them as angel bones.
The scapula, strangely shaped.
I had been fond of them
ever since, loved to
reach behind and feel
my own, loved to wrap my
arm around a girl and
feel the jut of hers through
her thin shirt.

She grabbed a fistful
of her feathers, ivory and
cream, lace and eggshell,
and paused there
for a moment, as if
she was just going to
feel them between her
fingers, nothing more and
certainly nothing less.
In that moment,
I could feel my own
breath leaving my
body like a soul.
It didn't last.
With a wrenching cry
she ripped and tugged,
heaving out the feathers
by the handful.
Pinpricks of blood
rose up in the empty
spaces the quills had
left behind. Tiny
red berries. I wanted to
lick them, cover
them with a tissue, forget that
I had ever seen them.
She kept going, tearing and
howling. The feathers
littered my floor, still

white – they had been
torn out of her too quickly
for her blood to stain
them. It stained her
instead. It stained me.
Next came her dress, also ivory
and definitely not lace.
She struggled out of it,
somehow – miraculously –
without smearing it
with the feather-blood.
It puddled onto the floor,
a pearlescent pool.
I wish she had tidied
the feathers into a pile,
ordered to face the same
way as each other,
ordered by size, maybe.
The fluffy down feathers
here, the water-proof
flight feathers there.
I wish she had hung the
dress up in my wardrobe
instead of letting
it crumple there.
She did what she did.
I watched all of it.

IX.

We look at the stars,
suspended balls of gas and fire burning
in enormous isolation,
and say: "Look, a bear! A crab! A belt!"
It is the very endearing need to humanize something
that exists on a scale we cannot
even comprehend.
We take something millions of light years away
and mold it into something
we can understand,
constellations with names that make sense to us,
pretending they look like something we have seen
before.
A bear. A crab. A belt.
This is how stargazing becomes a romantic activity,
the existential dread removed,
an opportunity to talk about how small we feel
and how big the universe is.
Lying next to you, I imagined gravity letting us go,
how we would look,
falling hand-in-hand into the sea of stars.
Would a cosmic net catch us? Would we fall into the
outstretched paws of Ursa Major?

How many of the stars we saw still existed,
and how many of them were just a shadow of old
light
that we could somehow still see?
I must have wondered this out loud
because you laughed, and it lingered visibly
in the cold air.
"I think that we matter to the universe," you said
finally. "I don't feel so small next to you."

X.

If you lean over me
and look into the dark
empty well of my heart
you won't even see
your reflection on
the surface.
I am completely
bottomless. Full
but very far away
from you.

Doesn't every well
dry up one day,
you ask me.
Won't you be dry
one day? Won't
you be empty, too?

I looked at you
very hard. I could
tell that you wanted
to drop a coin to
the bottom of me,
make a wish, hear
it clang and clatter.

A gold coin is a
small price to pay
for the far-fetched
chance that it
might work. Might
come true, after
all this time.

No, I said out loud.
Your coin would
never see the sun
again,
and I would keep
your wish inside me
forever.

Anything you give
to me, I will
swallow it whole,
and carry it with
me for the rest
of my life.

XI.

I do not comprehend the roar of the wake.
Who am I now?
We're all borrowed names
For the jousting of an empty hull.
We float in a spacious water,
Thrown together by chance and history.
At some point my lips open
And I become a blind man's poem.
When she comes to read me,
Is this death or life?

XII.

You will close yourself off
to all of the possibilities for intimacy,
horrified by the reality that someone
you no longer love will still know you
or at least know who you
were in a moment when
you loved them, too.
      They were physically close,
a deer pausing for a moment to drink from
a watering hole, big prey eyes
fluttering closed for a moment.
      A temporary sense of security.
They were able to study you like
a naturalist, notebook scribbles, sketches
of life. To know you is to capture you.

XIII.

While you testified against me,
I stood and watched.
I wasn't trying to make a
statement. I just wanted to be
able to see your eyes; the color
of rainwater on metal, ringed
by unapologetic eyelashes.
Your eyebrows pulled together
into a deliberate display of
sincerity. You told the judge
that you saw me there;
I was wearing a black cloak,
my face bared to the moon,
and I was holding
hands with the others, laughing
with glee around a cauldron or
a fire or a carcass or a shrine.
You saw me hold up a silver
blade that glittered and gleamed
and then I held it to the throat
of something to sacrifice, you
think it was a lamb, or was it
a turkey or a goat or a bawling
human child? (It was a deer,
a spotted fawn, three days old.)

And the blood rained down and
soaked into the grass, as dark
as the dew, and the trees drank
it up for they were very thirsty.
I was dancing as if nothing else
mattered and I looked you dead
in your iron-filing eyes and then
bared every one of my sharp
teeth. The judge never asked
you the one thing I wanted to
know, the words my tender
mouth could not quite form:
on that moonlit night
where you saw me:
why were you there,
in those woods, in Salem?
Why didn't you dance with us?

XIV.

Act of taking: to be needy,
to want, to commit the sins of jealousy
or of lust. Always ashamed to require something
from anyone, even a necessity – even worse
than taking is to
need.

Instead, the act of giving: it is
a disguise masquerading as generosity,
as virtue. The behavior of someone afraid
to want, to sin, to need,
afraid even once to need something
and have it be denied.

XV.

The things of the largest
value are ones that
I can roll over like a peach stone
in my mouth
without any sharp edges
to cut myself on.
No twinge of guilt,
sour tang of old sadness.
Some of these are
excruciatingly simple.
Cold, wet morning sunlight
that has never even thought
of burning, just
catches and glimmers on leaves.
Childhood sunlight, I mean.
Early morning excitement,
the only part of
the memory that I can
really trust.
It all seemed enormous
to me back then;
blades of grass that wrapped
around my feet as if
to pull them into the ground.
The monumental effort
of hauling myself onto

the lowest branch
of a tree, scratching
my shins against the bark,
heart pounding with
the fear of a fall that would
never have even broken
one of my bones,
would have barely even bruised me.
I enter the bedroom
I grow up in and feel this
change very deeply.
A bed that once felt
like it could be full of
monsters now can't even
be full of half of me.
My head overhangs the end,
my feet splay past the mattress.
Sometimes it still feels
like the bed, the tree, the
grass all shrunk
and I never grew.
Back to the sunlight,
it is something that I keep
to hold, inside my pocket,
to clutch tightly
against the palm of my hand
in the rolls and tumbles

of being an adult.
When I was a child I had
this infuriating habit
of watching the same movie
over and over again;
The Wizard of Oz.
I knew how it ended,
I knew every line
and the fact that none of it
would ever change
both shocked and reassured me.
As I roll those memories
over and over in my mouth,
I realize that I have not
let go of this habit,
just changed it to fit
what my life is now.
The list of things that can never
hurt me is small but concrete.
Well-worn, well-cherished.

XVI.

This is what we evolved for. Wonder of archaeology, digging up
fossilized bones to wonder at their circular lacunae, lakes of bone
to prove that weight was once distributed here. Muscle once attached
here, and here, and pulled, and blood ran through it until it ran dry.
I believe I can imagine what you looked like standing up, before
these bones collapsed into a primeval swamp.
I project my own wants onto what is left of you,
what color you were, what sound you perhaps would have made and what
way you walked while you made it. Galloping or meandering,
prairies or deserts. Did you lay eggs? Did you raise your own young
or leave them to fend for themselves?
Did you love?
Did you know you existed?

XVII.

You are a living mind on a dying tongue.
The hour has come.
The lady is dead.
The country is blackened
With dust and fire and shame.
Yet your memory
Will not die.
The harvest has come.
The night has come.
Now I sing for the memory of all.

Winter Solstice

I.

The first thing you ever fell in love with was your own melancholy. The empty hole that ached inside of you like a missing milk tooth, there for you to run your tongue over every few seconds in a constant reminder of something that was missing from you. Every time you held your gaze in the mirror and looked more deeply into that dark hole, in return, it looked more deeply back at you. The luminescent circles around your pupils became bluer and bluer until it leaked out and pumped through your tangled veins. Until all of you bled an empty aching blue.

II.

The children die first, some howls
and some pangs and tears,
then the adults.
Then my wife, the harp of the whole land,
falling to the ground in pain.
That sound is the death bell.
The people are singing and lamenting;
but their cries of pain
have no path.
They fight each other
then slowly they lose courage.
They turn against each other.
And soon each one will call for his own blood.
I sing, but they do not hear.
The waters of the dry plain are burning
and their flames rise like distant laughter.
In a waste hewn out of cliffs where the earth burns
you cannot see the doom of the city.
Did you not hear it the first time?
Those who heard it the first time, did
you not watch the disaster as it arrived?

III.

What's your
fascination with
pretty dead girls?
You know what I mean,
It's how the mystery
      novels always
      begin.
It's never an old man
naked, withered under
the sun or (even sexier)
the frigid winter snow.
It is a young girl,
her skin porcelain,
feigning untouched
except for blue and purple
blossoming, blooming.
      A metaphor
for crushed berries,
crushed flowers.
Usually, her blood
is hardly spilled, still
      waiting
      inside her
for something interesting
to happen, not knowing

that the most interesting
thing already has.
What's your
fascination with
pretty dead girls?
The snow catches in her
eyelashes, glittering like
crystals. Her lips painted
deepest purple, a color
that has never known
pink or warm.
Perhaps some of her
is covered by the snow,
a make-believe gown of
fairy-tale snow white.
She is such an enticing
start to your story,
          such a
          page turner.
We wanted to know
who killed her,
how she died.
Hand around the throat
almost always, bullet
to the head almost
never. Stab wound
          sometimes

      if unlucky.
Was she
always this pretty, you
know, when she was
alive? Or is she just
pretty now that she
has joined the ranks
of pretty dead girls?

IV.

The mercy I begged for
ended up just being
a crude metal cage
I welded around my heart.
The craftmanship was
ugly,
but it was strong enough
to stifle its rhythm
without stopping it from
beating altogether.
60 beats per minute,
anything more
is a waste.
I wanted to live
without feeling.
I still do.

V.

My eyes moved slowly,
so I could feign innocence
as I read the secret symbols of your body.
Your silence was a feast on a winter's night,
a view to die for.
"Have I found you?"
You breathed, but did not say.

"I am inside of you," I whispered.
"There are things inside of you, too,"
you whispered back, laughing.
"That's how it is with you and me."

Your world exists in the hearts of all living things.
When I walked through the door
into your life
it was not so easily claimed.

VI.

Even on my death bed
I will sing again in the snow.
A snow drop, shedding a perfect blossom
in a field of grey grasses,
undeterred by the wind
that sweeps across the plain.
The steam of my breath
will fill the evening air.

Departing, I rest.
Satisfied, I can rest.

What does a life amount to?
There is no way to tell.
Just what I make it seem like,
about that life.
It's a fine life.
Pity that I have to leave it behind.

Long after the winter flowers have faded,
the daisies will bloom, brightening the plain.
They will tell me where to look.

VII.

I keep it all inside my body,
scratching at the door,
at the aortic arch,
begging to go outside.

It does want to get out,
it does ask for it,
demand it, scratching and scrabbling.
I feel the way it wants to run
through the woods and the valleys
covered in icy moonlight.
Leaving carnage behind,
claw marks and carrion.
If I let it out,
seawater will flood in
and fill the space it left,
making me infinitely heavy,
sinking me down
so that I can't chase after
the thing I have let
loose in the woods.

VIII.

Standing on sea-slick mud
My eyes look to the dark waves.
My eyes are all they see.
It is no good for mortal heart to pause
In your deep, quiet murmur.

I can hear you talking to me.
I close my eyes and I put on
A color of your flesh, and a color of mine,
By slow compulsion.
We move round and round in these contortions,
And the wind-driven waves, like the arms
Of a dead statue, cry from one shore to the other.

Pale is the morning now.
My god of the darkness, sleep it!
Stones, black with sea-foam, sigh
In the shadow of the driftwood.

Don't give way.
I am nearly submerged.

IX.

Tried so hard to get closer to you;
sidling up gently, slowly so as not to
alarm. I wanted to be so close that I lived
inside of you, right next to your heart,
ribs wrapped around me like the arms
of a lover. Without noticing I tried
so hard to get close to you that I passed
straight through, like you were a ghost
and there I was on the other side of
your body with only the muscle
memory of how your ribs felt,
and not a single kiss to show for it.

X.

I have always wondered about
the moment in death
when there stops being
two people in the room.
The moment when you are left
alone.
      I don't know if it is
the last breath or the first
moment without one.
The final heartbeat?
When it starts to slow?
      Do the brain waves stop
before all of this? Or after?
I want to know at which
point in my sentence
I was talking to you
      and at which point
I was, in a cool chemical room
with lights that made my skin
look green, talking
      only to myself.

XI.

Among this rot you sleep, old god?
There lies a human birth
That long years will not waken.
Yet you cling, though with your hands
You cannot clasp the body,
Untended and abandoned, to a dead tyrant.

Speak, you beast. Cogitate, you thrum.
Do you even dream, now?
Silent is your sight, as in the church of sleep.
You are the watcher, not of the dead,
Yet you are deaf to all their pleas,
And evil lies with you of an eternal kind.
Your giant red chest
Glitters with the weight of flesh.
Here lies a brute.

And here are you still, this dead tyrant,
Such as he who at night,
A cloaked thief, accosts the swan,
And eats the kill.

Look you, old god, speak.
As long as your skull and jaws stay
Obscured, I think it has not been long
Since your eyes were open in a dream,

To see your defiled corpse,
Hanging here upon this tree.
The gray shapelessness of your skin
Like a fat slumbering beast, the limp
Of your hard bones, the few tufts of white hair
And some black spots that grace you as one
With a faint tattoo, so fades before me.

XII.

This is my worm now: is it murder? Is it beast?
What will be the soil, in which I will rot?
This is death,
and the world where I come from is life.
If I cannot fly, I will sink.
Here, in this breeze, I smell the stink of decay.
I am, in short, doomed.

XIII.

Bones under the ground, collected in small piles
that make a quiet mockery of what they used to
be. A dog collapsed, skull imprisoned in ribcage,
claws littering the earth like seeds that will never
grow. Roots where whiskers used to be. Rows of
teeth and jawbones to clatter back and forth, one
skeleton to another. How are you? Where are you,
I can't see anything – isn't it dark here? How odd
for a once-nocturnal animal to be reduced to this,
to a perpetual lack of light. A forever blindness.
The bones touch the damp soil, the worms and
beetles that crawl and writhe, the mysterious
mushrooms sprouting where no light will ever touch
them. Some things feed off rot and decay, and other
things create it. Symbiosis is the most pure and
untouchable type of love. It gives and it takes. Six
feet under the surface, two femurs sigh together,
pushed into each other by a hundred years of the
world spinning on its axis. The skull and crossbones,
the X that marks the spot, right there in
an unremarkable and certainly unmarked grave.

XIV.

What is worse?
Not seeing or not
touching? I think
that physical
memory lasts
longer, the feeling
of something against
your skin lingers
longer than the
sight of it. It only
takes days of not
seeing someone
for me to forget
what their small
details look like.
When I imagine
them, they look
like a stranger
seen across the
road, enough to
make out the
general details
of the face but
I get some things
wrong, like the

angle of the nose,
the shade of the
eyes. After longer
than that, it gets
more warped –
expressionist ideas,
the vague notion
of dark eyebrows,
cheekbones, ears.
A shadow behind
a mirror, behind
frosted glass.
They are both as
bad as each other
but one lasts
longer, hits harder,
bites deeper.

XV.

My brain goes faster than my body can
deal with, stumbling
into things.
I am always outside of my own orbit
existing in limbo or in mania.
I'm not sure if gravity has any
effect here.
You reach out to touch me and
your own atmosphere extends to
encompass my failed planet, providing a
gravitational field.
It has exactly the right percentage
of oxygen and nitrogen to sustain
life, evolution, to produce rain.
It slows me down,
brain and body are married again.
Lungs can breathe enough,
words come out unsure but in the right order.
We orbit each other, like neighboring
planets or maybe like I am a moon,
a tamed asteroid now circling loyally
as if on a leash.
Even in sleep I feel your gravity.

XVI.

In your heart there lives
an animal wounded, an animal bleeding.
      You open a door and
show her to me, writhing. I reach for it.
You grieve your own kindness, I imagine
burying the animal, imagine the shovel
      and the graveyard.
Instead the animal warms to the faint concept
of my touch, of my hands
      and I domesticate you.
      I teach you how to be gentle.

XVII.

I never managed to stifle
the deep, penetrating
itch of caring for you.
The pot on the stove
boiled over,
coating everything
around it in something
too difficult to scrub off,
and then
          slowly
it went cold.

Tron lives.

Coming Soon by Brandon Tezzano

Indigo Musings
Witch Trials
Drops of Grey
Realms of the Afterlife
He Who Dwells in the Abyss
The Prophecies
Cybertronic Oracle
You Were Wrong About Me
The Morphean Labyrinth
Shadow Ruminations

About the Author

Brandon Tezzano lives in Baltimore, Maryland. When he is not writing perplexing literature, he creates music, films, and digital paintings. He holds degrees in English and Film, and is currently pursuing a Doctorate.